The Tears Will Cease: Recovery from Dissociative Identity Disorder

Shirley J. Davis
And
Jessica J. Baker

Dedicated to my good friend Jessica J. Baker whose help made writing this book possible.

The Beginning of Therapy
The Memories Return

Normally when humans become frightened they will secrete specialized hormones into their bodies to ready them both physically and mentally for fight, flight or freeze. Then, after the danger has passed, these very important hormones will drain away. In horribly abused children who are under constant threat, however, these chemicals never completely drain and their developing brains become unable to process memory correctly. (In fact, the amygdalae and hippocampi, the regions responsible for processing and storing of memories, of adult survivors are often smaller in volume.) As a result of these brain changes, memories of abuse can become compartmentalized and split off from the conscious. Later in life, (usually between ages 30-40 depending on your DNA makeup), human brains mature and those memories once kept separate are suddenly accessible and tend to surface on their own. This can cause havoc to the emotional health of the survivor.

The phenomenon of being flooded by memories can be compared to vomiting as the things that have been forgotten are relived, via flashbacks, unbidden and without warning. Because these memories are so disturbing, it is important to learn and practice coping skills to mitigate their effects on the survivor's life.

Author's Personal Perspective:

When I first began to recovery the memories of what happened to me as a child was overwhelmed with emotions and thoughts and physical sensations. I began to do research online to help me understand why I was remembering these things now (I was 30) and felt quite relieved when I learned that I wasn't weird, but that my brain had reached a point of maturity.

Before long, I realized I could not handle the emotional turmoil I was experiencing, so I sought help. I found a great Therapist and we began my trip down the road less traveled.

My Therapist began to help me learn techniques and skills to calm myself down such as coloring, painting, and reading. She taught me that I needed to climb out of my trauma and take a vacation from myself.

The Memories Return

Question 1:

What did you learn about how human brains function? Had you ever thought of your brain as being fundamentally different from others who have not experienced severe abuse as children?

Question 2:

Do you believe it is time (if you have not already) to seek the help of a Professional?

Question 3:

What kinds of things are you doing to help calm down and to take a vacation from yourself?

Author's Suggestions

Question 1

Stress hormones are a normal part of how the human brain handles danger; Stress hormones are responsible for getting our bodies ready for fight, flight or freeze; The brains of people who have been severely abused have been altered by these hormones.

Question 2

I would wholeheartedly suggest that anyone who is reading this book and is recovering from severe trauma issues to seek the help of a competent Therapist.

Question 3

- Writing in a journal or a short story
- Taking long walks outdoors
- Watching a funny movie
- There are any number of positive and uplifting things to do!

Living in Chaos

Living in total chaos is the hardest part of recovering from severe trauma. The alters that once protected the person have now become a liability as they do things without their knowledge that are socially unacceptable.

A good example may be that as small children, the survivor was forced to steal food and money to survive. Now that they are grown, these behaviors are no longer necessary. Unfortunately, those parts of may be stuck in what is termed trauma-time and do not understand that they are a grown person. As a result, they are still acting out and getting in trouble, possibly even bad trouble.

The trick is to find ways to work WITH the alters not fight against them. They ARE NOT the enemy, rather they are parts who are hurt and wanting children in need of love and kindness. Learning to treat these parts with the respect and caring that all children deserve is a huge step towards healing.

Author's Personal Perspective:

I once lived in a very small apartment and one or more of my alters decided it was necessary to get up in the night and rummage for food. The problem was I was getting black and blue from running into things. My therapist suggested I make a peanut butter sandwich and leave it where whoever was sleepwalking could find it. I did so, and I would wake up in the morning to find the sandwich gone. The bruising also disappeared. In this way, I was working WITH the needs of my alters, not against them.

Living in Chaos

Question 1:

How would you describe the chaos you have been experiencing since beginning to recover the memories of what happened to you?

Question 2:

How can you "work with" your alters instead of against them?

Question 3:

Can you list three things you can do that can lessen the effects of trauma-time on now-time?

Author's Suggestions:

Question 1:

- Spending money you don't have
- Saying things you don't remember
- Losing things.

Question 2:

- Recognize they are not the enemy
- Begin to understand that they are hurting children
- Learning to love the alters as parts of yourself.

Question 3:

- Seek the help of a Therapist
- Budget money for alters to spend
- Spend time getting to know the needs of the alters.

The Days of Needing Help

No one wants to admit they had horrible things happen to them in childhood, let alone face the horrible flashbacks with their accompanying emotions that seem to come out of nowhere. The overwhelming feelings of hopelessness and despair can be daunting. That's why it was implied in the last section that if one wishes to conquer the chaos in their life brought on by recovery from severe childhood trauma, a Therapist must be sought. this cannot be stressed enough.

Unfortunately, there is a lot of confusion and myth surrounding psychotherapy. One prevailing attitude is that people who seek out a therapist are weak and should just "buck up" or "pull themselves together". Society tends to stigmatize people who seek out therapy thinking that only crazy folks need this type of assistance. Nothing can be farther from the truth. When faced with the overwhelming knowledge that people who should have loved and cherished the survivor as children, instead used them for their own needs an objective outside voice of reason is needed to help navigate the deep and disturbing waters of recovery.

Accepting help from a qualified professional is another important step forward.

Author's Personal Perspective:

At first, I didn't understand what was happening to me and behaviors that I had always put off to a bad memory (losing time) I found myself mired me down in the mud slide of flashbacks and emotions. I could barely function. It became apparent to me that I needed help if I was going to make any sense out of the things that I was becoming aware of, so I sought out a therapist.

My family and friends didn't like the idea of me talking to a stranger about "family matters" and they tried their best to dissuade me from seeking help. The stigma of being related to or a friend of a "crazy person" clouded the need for me to be happy and well. I was asked why I didn't just "move on" and leave my past in the past. I wish it could have been that easy! The fact is, once these emotions and memories began to surface I couldn't stop them, so the only solution was to seek help.

I was lucky. I found the perfect match the first try.

I live in a small rural community so finding a competent therapist who could help me with my intense needs could have proven difficult. I was very fortunate to have found a great match on my first try. My advice, if you don't make a good match, keep trying. You don't have to "settle" for someone who does not believe you or in your ability to heal.

The days of Needing Help

Question 1:

Have you considered your need of a therapist to help you understand and cope with the emotions you are experiencing due to childhood trauma?

Question 2:

What erroneous thoughts about psychotherapy keeps (kept) you from seeking help?

Question 3:

Have you experienced any negative feedback from your family or because you wish to seek the help of a therapist?

Author's Suggestions

Question 1

As I stated in this chapter, in my opinion it is impossible to face these issues on one's own. A competent therapist is a must.

Question 2

- Only crazy people need therapy
- I should just move on and forget
- I should "buck up".

Question 3

Some stigma must be expected. Society has strange notions about what psychotherapy is and is not. Don't' be misled by negative feedback from others. If you need help, please get it.

The Dangerous Stage

The emotions that have begun to surface can be very strong, and often survivor's find themselves in the position of feeling self-destructive. This is a very serious consequence of working on the tough issues of childhood abuse, let along working on the problems involved with living with Dissociative Identity Disorder.

It isn't hard to understand why one may have these extreme thoughts. Many times, as children, we were taught that telling someone what was going on was wrong or we may have been threatened with harm if we told. Also, we may have been convinced by our abusers that the abuse was our fault.

Sometimes a survivor may feel they are dirty or ugly. They may feel that no one will ever want them romantically because of the horrendous things that were done to their bodies.

In a way, it is like survivors were programmed to self-destruct. It takes hard work and a good therapist to carefully work through the maze of these powerful errant thoughts.

Please, if you feel these feelings or have thoughts of self-harm please get assistance as soon as possible. Don't ignore those thoughts thinking they mean nothing and that nothing bad will happen to you.

Author's Personal Perspective:

In 1995 I took an overdose of pills that nearly ended my journey. It was not planned, but one of my alters was feeling self-destructive and the next thing I knew I had taken three bottles of pills. I thank God that my personality Bianca, who is a tenacious eighteen-year old girl, was not affected immediately as was I by the drugs and was able to call for help. The suddenness of this decision to end my existence startled and frightened me. My therapist and I immediately began to work on inner communication so that I could know and recognize the warning signs should someone inside become suicidal.

If you feel overwhelmed, seek help and do not be afraid of admitting to yourself and someone else what you need. If you need time in the hospital, do not be afraid to go there. There is real danger in this stage of recovery, remember that.

Keep a list of emergency names and numbers that everyone in your system can find and use should you begin to lose control.

The Dangerous Stage

Question 1:

Identity two emotions you are experiencing that are connected to the memories that you have had surface.

Question 2:

Identify two thoughts that cause you to want to self-destruct.

Question 3:

Make a list and keep easily accessible some phone numbers you can call if you find yourself overwhelmed and feeling like self-harming or suicidal. (I'm leaving you an empty page to write these down)

List of Emergency Numbers

Author's Suggestions

Question 1:

- Fear
- Self-loathing
- Helplessness
- Loneliness
- Disbelief.

Question 2:

- I am dirty
- I am not worthy of life
- I should die
- I am lying
- I'm making all of this stuff up.

Question 3:

List the numbers of local and national Suicide Prevention Hotlines, your therapist, friends, local hospitals, to name a few.

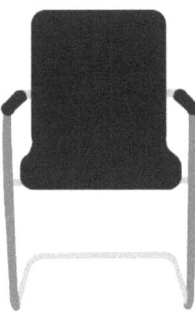

Therapy
It's Your Dime

Therapy is a unique experience to say the least. People have all kinds of misconceptions about what it is and what it isn't. One is usually confused and frustrated from lack of understanding of why the therapist doesn't just give them a set of instructions or directions as to what to do. A good and well-trained therapist will not give advice, that's simply not their job. Their job is to be a kind of seeing eye dog. They guide their clients through the maze of their pasts into the beauty of the present. Therapy is not a place to get directions as to how to live life, instead therapy is a process where a person faces their past head on. With the help of a trained person the past can be laid to rest so that it no longer rules every waking moment.

The things revealed to the therapist are very frightening at first, mainly because in the past many survivors were warned never to tell anyone about what went on behind closed doors. It is this secrecy, however, that holds them hostage. It feels strange to sit for an hour and talk to a total stranger about intimate things that you were told never to reveal to anyone "or else". Trust is hard for people who have been treated so horribly, so choose your therapist wisely but be sure to give him or her a chance.

Another important thing to remember is that a well-trained therapist will not take the lead in the sessions, rather they will follow their clients. In other words, if one wishes to spend the hour talking about the weather or playing coy games, the therapist will patiently allow this. After all, it is the client's hour and their dime. Sometimes a client will spend a large amount of time, at first, talking about

Author's Personal Perspective

I remember clearly feeling that my therapist should just give me the answers or a list of steps to follow so that I could get well quickly. The reality is that recovery from severe trauma takes time and my therapist's job wasn't to give me the answers but to help me to better understand what happened to me so that I could finally put the past in the past where it belongs.

I felt fearful deep inside of telling my therapist about the things that had happened to me, or the way those things made me feel then and now. I would go into her office and either space out or talk about "nothing". She didn't lose patience, instead she kept patiently encouraging me along. Slowly, achingly slowly, I began to trust her. It took me two before I could cry in front of my therapist. On the day I did, she stated that she usually judged her client's getting well by the fact they stop crying, but me she judged by the fact I had begun.

Therapy
It's Your Dime

Question 1:

What expectations do you have of your therapist and therapy?

Question 2:

Write a list of three changes you would to see in yourself and your life in the future after therapy.

Question 3:

List four ways you can be good to yourself that are positive and uplifting.

Author's Suggestions:

Question 1:

- That the therapist would have all the answers
- That the problems presented to the therapist can be answered quickly
- That all a person needs to do is follow a set of steps and all these issues will be resolved.

Question 2:

- I will feel calm
- I will know peace
- I will feel happy
- I will return to school.

Question 3:

- Get plenty of sleep
- Eat well
- Take medications as prescribed
- See your Medical Doctor regularly.

Getting and Staying Grounded

The emotions experienced by a survivor in recovery are extreme to say the least. Deep seated fears from childhood may surface and many find themselves having **flashbacks**, practicing **avoidance behaviors** and having **panic attacks**. This is totally normal and understandable, but exhausting. Bedtime and nighttime often become things survivors dread because when they were small their beds were where they were the most vulnerable.

In the next three chapters I am going to break down the above statement into bite-sized nuggets. I know it may seem I am going to spend a great deal of time speaking about these subjects, but it is important to understand them to get and stay grounded.

Flashbacks

A flashback is re-experiencing something traumatic which happened, sometimes decades before, as though it were happening in the now. The person experiencing a flashback can see, taste, smell and feel the emotions they had when the traumatic event occurred. Flashbacks can happen suddenly, usually being brought on by an external trigger such as an odor or a sound. It makes sense that triggers would be so powerful as all humans process memories for recall using the five senses for a reference. (For instance, the smell of fresh baked bread may remind one of a warm memory of a favorite Grandparent or favorite day.) The difference between regular recall and a flashback is that the latter is disruptive to the lives of the person experiencing them. They are frightening and sometimes the sufferer will thrash out, or in the case of a person living with DID, cause one to dissociate into an alter who may not live in enough reality to behave normally. This often greatly complicates the lives of people, making holding a job or having a meaningful relationship nearly or totally impossible.

One way to handle these intrusive memories is to practice grounding techniques. These techniques allow the brain to break away from the trauma-time memory and return to the now.

I have made a short list of the most commonly used grounding techniques. There are many more, one needs to choose the one that works the best for them.

If possible, say out loud to yourself the following questions (If you cannot speak out loud, then say them in your mind):

- Where am I?
- What is today?
- What is the date?
- What is the month?
- What is the year?
- How old am I?
- What season is it?

Physical sensations are important to grounding ourselves. Try doing some of the following:

- Hold a pillow or stuffed animal.
- Hold a piece of ice in your hand.
- Listen to music.
- Name 2 things you can see in the room with you.
- Name 2 things you can hear right now.
- Pay attention to the movement of your abdomen as you breathe.

Sometimes a Visual reminder is needed to help stay grounded. Keep these items with you or within sight:

- Pictures of important people in your life today.
- A calendar with the current month and year.
- A locket with a picture of someone important in today.

Author's Personal Perspective:

I once had a horrendous fear of the shower because just turning on the water would cause me to relive (flash back) to memories of abuse. One must be clean so I knew I needed to find a technique that would help me. On my own I thought up and utilized this technique. I bought a calendar with the current year printed in large, easy-to-see numbers at the top, then put it in waterproof plastic and hung it from the shower head. This way, whenever I would take a shower and felt a flashback to childhood abuse coming on, I would look at that calendar and it would help me orient myself to the reality that I was not back in the 1960s, where I was a helpless child, but in the year written in bold numbers at the top.

On an encouraging note, I would like to add that I've noticed as time has passed and I've worked on these issues that using grounding techniques has become automatic and usually it takes much less time and effort for me to be reoriented to time and place than it did when I first began treatment.

Flashbacks

Question 1:

Pin point and write two triggers that can cause you to experience a flashback.

Question 2:

Name two ways that flashbacks are interfering with your life.

Question 3:

What two techniques can you think of to add to the above list?

Author's Suggestions:

Question 1:

Triggers can be just about anything. Think of the senses; taste, touch, smell, sight, and sound.

Question 2:

- Panic attacks
- Lost wages
- Social embarrassment
- Inability to concentrate, etc.

Question 3:

Remember, the list I gave is only an example of some of the things I have used. Use your imagination.

Avoidance Behaviors

Avoidance behaviors are based on the need to avoid or escape thoughts or feelings. Some of the behaviors utilized include **avoidance strategy** and **conflict prevention**.

Below is a partial list of common avoidance behaviors:

- Dropping a class rather than give a speech

- Changing jobs to avoid real or imagined conflict

- Leaving a gathering early to avoid being triggered

- Hiding in the restroom at a fun event to avoid the chance of being noticed

- Avoiding eye contact to avoid being asked a question

- Drinking or doing drugs to avoid strong emotions

- Sitting in the back of a classroom to avoid being asked a question because of a fear one may not know the answer to or give the wrong answer.

Avoidance strategy seeks to put off conflict indefinitely by delaying or ignoring the conflict. In this way, the avoider hopes the problem resolves itself without a confrontation and simply goes away.

Conflict prevention is a method of attempting to avoid direct confrontation of the issue at hand using methods such as changing the subject, putting off a discussion until later, or simply not bringing up the subject that can cause the conflict at all. Procrastination is the most commonly used conflict prevention method.

One must keep in mind that everyone utilizes avoidance behaviors, it is a normal part of being human. These behaviors are only detrimental when they get in the way of normal functioning and cause distress, such as substance abuse or interpersonal relationship difficulties.

While it is easy to understand why a person who has lived through severe child abuse would practice avoidance behaviors, (as helpless children, survivors looked for ways to help them make sense out of the chaos that was being perpetrated against them), it is important to note that these behaviors are harmful. They undermine self-esteem and don't allow people to face life. Instead, avoidance behaviors make running away from uncomfortable situations the norm and when a person is facing the hard work involved with psychotherapy, they can prolong recovery. (cancelling appointments or spacing out to avoid talking about difficult memories or emotions for example can stretch out the time it takes to heal)

It may seem counter-intuitive, but the best way to end abuse of avoidance behaviors is to face the feared situation head-on. To be sure, this is a very uncomfortable thing to do, but to keep on allowing oneself to continue to avoid something because it reminds of childhood lives is to continue to give away power to those who harmed us.

Some of the 12-step groups have two slogans I like very much.

"The only way out is through."

And

"Face Every Problem and Recover"

Author's Personal Perspective:

By delaying talking about something as important as strong emotions or memories, I know I lost some valuable time with my therapist. I would enter her office and try all I could to steer her and myself away from the important topics that needed to be discussed. I think I was afraid of the pain and that I would start crying and never stop. Bottom line, I didn't want to lose control and be real in front of her. This slowed my progress way down. After I overcame my fear of being myself before her and I began to cry my recovery began in earnest.

Avoidance Behavior

Question 1:

Name an avoidance behavior you have used in the recent past.
What you were trying to avoid feeling? Why do you believe you
felt the need to use this behavior?

Question 2:

How has using this avoidance behavior negatively affected your
life?

Question 3:

In what way can you face this problem head-on? Do you believe
doing this will help speed up your recovery time? Why?

Author's Suggestions:

Question 1:

In my perspective, I used the conflict prevention methods of putting off talking about the subject of a memory or emotion or changing the subject. I was trying to avoid feeling out of control and vulnerable with my therapist. I used this behavior to prevent myself from feeling helpless like I did when I was a small child.

Question 2:

By playing little mind games with my therapist, I in turn kept myself imprisoned by the strong emotions that she could have supported me with. I also delayed my healing.

Question 3:

I began to force myself to talk about what emotions and memories were plaguing me and dealing with the fear of doing so. It wasn't easy, and it took time. By talking about the abuse, I had endured, and its lasting effects, I sped up my recovery time enormously. I think my healing sped up because I was taking power back from my abusers by letting go of the secrecy they had imposed upon me. A secret can be a very powerful prison.

Panic Attacks

A panic attack is a sudden episode of intense fear that triggers severe physical reactions when there is no real danger or apparent cause. These attacks can be very frightening and disruptive to a person's life. When first experienced, one might think they are losing control or having a heart attack.

Symptoms Can Include:

- Palpitations
- Pounding heart,
- Sweating
- Trembling or shaking
- Sensations of shortness of breath or smothering
- Feelings of choking
- Chest pain or discomfort
- Nausea or abdominal distress
- Feeling dizzy, unsteady, light-headed, or faint
- Chills or heat sensations
- Numbness or tingling sensations
- De-realization (feelings of unreality)
- Depersonalization (being detached from oneself)
- Fear of losing control or "going crazy"
- Fear of dying
- Dissociation

Our bodies are equipped with a marvelous coping mechanism to keep us safe in the face of danger. This is our fight or flight response. When we perceive danger through one or more of our senses the primitive brain, that which controls our automatic responses, takes over from our thinking or cognitive brain and sends out signals to our heart, lungs, and other vital organs to ready us to turn and fight or flee. This evolutionary marvel in our skull does this by causing large amounts of adrenaline and other compounds to be dumped into our blood, and that is why we feel many of the above-mentioned symptoms.

As with flashbacks, this frightening phenomenon is usually precipitated by a trigger, such as a sight or smell, which reminds the sufferer of something that happened in their traumatic past. If you live with Dissociative Identity Disorder, you may find yourself coping by dissociating and allowing another personality to come forward and cope with the situation.

While panic attacks are horrible to experience, they are not in and of themselves dangerous.

In the next three paragraphs are some very good coping techniques one can use to bring the frequency of panic attacks and their effects on one's life under control.

Relaxing and taking slow, deep and complete breathes helps by pulling the mind away from the perceived danger from the past and grounding it in the now. Slow, deep and complete breathes will also help to reverse the release of adrenaline and other stress hormones into the blood.

Stopping the emergency message that is being sent by your primitive brain as a result of a trigger is vital. One possible way is to shout the word "STOP!". Obviously, there are situations where this will be embarrassing, but so will be the outcome of having to leave or acting out if one can't get the panic attack under control. By interrupting the emergency message, one ends the loop of the same catastrophic thoughts from cascading over and over again and gives one a chance to calm down.

Using a pre-chosen statement can also slow or stop a panic attack. When one realizes that a panic attack is begin brought on by a negative statement repeating itself and triggering the fight or flight response in our brains, one can then plan strong opposing messages to say when a panic attack strikes.

Author's Personal Perspective

I am aware of most of the triggers that can cause me to experience a panic attack, yet I still get caught off guard once in a while. I have found that concentrating on my breathing and bringing it under control while replacing the emergency message playing in my mind extremely helpful. It simply isn't possible to be alert to every trigger, so pre-planning responses is very important.

Panic Attacks

Please use the following scenario to answer the questions for this section.

A woman survivor of severe child sexual abuse is in the middle of a busy department store shopping. While passing the aisle containing cologne she smells the scent of the cologne one of her childhood abusers used at the same time a child in a nearby shopping cart begins to cry. Her primitive brain suddenly perceives a threat to her person based on experiences she lived through long ago and begins to pump adrenaline into her blood to ready her for fight or flight. Suddenly, the woman feels her heart beating wildly and a horrible sense of impending doom.

Question 1:

What can the woman do to help bring her physical symptoms under control?

Question 2:

Can she use any verbal message to interrupt her panic attack? What words or simple phrases besides "STOP!" do you feel would help you in a similar situation?

Question 3:

What pre-chosen statement do you believe the woman could use? What pre-chosen statement would you use in a similar situation?

Author's Suggestions:

Question 1:

Concentrating on her breathing would help her brain to stop pumping adrenalin into her blood by breaking its concentration on the triggering event.

Question 2:

I have used the words and phrases such as: quit, it's alright, and it's happening today.

Question 3:

The phrase she could have used and that I have used can be, "that was then, this is now."

Creating a Safe Place

As a first step in getting to know one's internal system, (the alters), it is important to have a safe haven where all can feel safe. Since the alternate personalities are constructs of the mind, this place must be a mental location. The sky is the limit to the number and types of safe places one can imagine. Some places constructed by people in recovery from Dissociative Identity Disorder include warm sandy beaches, gently rolling meadows, rugged mountains, fields of flowers and forests.

The purpose of these safe havens is to give a neutral area, hidden away from the everyday stress of life, where communication between the alters can take place. Opening a dialogue between the members of one's internal system is vital to overcoming the major symptoms of DID, including the host losing time when another personality takes over. If the personality who wishes to take over has a place to vent their needs, then the waking self and the others can work out a compromise and solution preventing the splitting from taking place.

Having a dialogue within the alter system takes time to develop. At first all the alters may resist or mistrust the process, but after a time they find that meeting together in a safe place is very helpful and productive to meeting their needs.

Author's Personal Perspective:

I chose a warm and sandy beach as my safe place. It is a wonderful haven where the sun can't burn your skin, the water is so safe you can walk on it and the fire in the fire pit can't burn you. It is here that I sat for a long time and waited for my alters to come to me. Slowly, I was approached by them. The first was a three- year old named Mary Ellen. She came one evening, crawled into my lap and introduced herself. There have been many, many other introductions since and we regularly have meetings around the beach fire to discuss what is going on and how to solve internal problems. The creation of the beach has been a godsend, allowing me to discovery my past and the parts of myself that hold the memories of it.

Creating a Safe Place

Question 1:

What type of safe place would you like to construct in your mind?

Question 2:

What 2 goals would you like to achieve by building your safe place?

Question 3:

What would be the first thing you would want to say to an alter on your first meeting on in your safe place?

Author's Suggestions:

Question 1:

Be creative. You can build a safe place literally any place or in any time. You can be elaborate or simple in its design. It is up to your personal needs and desires.

Question 2:

Keep these goals simple at first. Some examples:

- Getting to know the names of your alters
- Understanding the emotional needs of the alters
- Gaining control over your days and nights

Question 3:

Hello is a nice start, but feel free to ask questions and treat the children like children and really listen to what they have to say.

Mothering

As anyone who lives with Dissociative Identity Disorder knows, it is very uncomfortable and destabilizing to be a mystery to one's self. It can seem as though someone or something else is in control of one's body and emotions when in reality, alternate personalities in one's system are aspects of the same person who are stuck in, what is termed, trauma-time. Their actions are often related directly to the severe abuse that occurred to the person sometimes decades earlier in their lives.

Often fear and anger are felt by the person who is given the diagnosis of DID for the existence of their alters, but it is important to remember that the others in one's system are not demons or horrible creatures bent on the destruction of the waking-self, rather they were created to save the waking-self from the knowing about the trauma so that they could continue living and remain sane. Once a person understands this basic fact, they can then begin to recognize their parts for what they are, hurting and lonely personalities who need nurturance and love. In other words, they need a mother.

In most instances, this position, that of a warm and compassionate mother, falls on the head of the waking-self. At first, this may cause a great deal of resentment for this personality. They may feel that a great injustice is being asked since they too feel the need to be mothered.

Anger is also common as the understanding of how they were cheated out of having a mother who would love and protect them in childhood emerges.

These emotions, resentment and anger are totally normal and will pass once the benefits of mothering the system have begun to be felt. Just what are the benefits of a person becoming the mother of their internal system? Here is just list of three things but there are many others.

- Better internal communication
- Peaceful coexistence
- Less fear
- Increased ability to control splitting

The best place for this internal mothering to begin is usually the safe place formed in the mind of the person living with Dissociative Identity Disorder.

Once mothering of the system is established the person living with DID is well on their way to recovery.

Author's Personal Perspective:

I indeed felt very angry and resentful at first at the knowledge that I had to become my own mother. It was after it was explained to me by my therapist that in the normal development of children into adults all humans become their own mothers, I stopped resisting. I learned quickly that my system is comprised of many hurting children. I saw them then not as enemies, but as dear friends. Since I had no frame of reference as to what a good mother looks like, I began to ask my therapist questions, pay attention when I saw mother's interacting with their children, and explore the internet looking for information. I even took a Child Psychology class at our local junior college.

I learned most of what I do with my children by trial and error, however, just like all human parents do. I play games, draw, color, and look through the toy section of the department store with my child alters. I go shopping and give a monetary allowance each month to my eighteen-year old self. There are tons of things that I can do to interact with my alters that are fun.

I also spend a great deal of time exploring with the alters their boo-boos which are very often related to the abuse that I survived as a child which they remember as though it were still happening today. I'll go to the beach and hold them, cuddle them, rock them and give them reassurance and love.

The benefits I have received from becoming my own mother are enormous. I have a much better ability to handle day to day experiences without splitting, thus the chaos I once lived in has died down. Also, I am more in tune with my own emotions, triggers and why I may be experiencing flashbacks.

Mothering

Question 1:

In what ways have your alters protected you from the trauma experiences of your past?

Question 2:

In your own words describe what a good mother looks like.

Question 3:

Name 3 things you can do to mother yourself.

Author's Suggestions

Question 1:

- Holding the memories until later in life
- Kept me sane
- Kept me alive

Question 2:

Use your imagination or search the internet. You can also ask questions of your friends or therapist. There are many ways to explore this subject.

Question 3:

- Buy yourself new clothes
- Take your older alters shopping
- Buy toys
- Color with crayons
- Finger paint
- Again, be creative!

Taking Responsibility

One of the most fear filled symptoms of DID is losing time. During this blacked-out period, a person living with this condition may do or say things that are harmful to others or themselves emotionally or physically. Sometimes the events that took place while the person was dissociated were illegal in nature. Due to the fact that one doesn't wish to believe they are capable of doing such things, it is very tempting for the waking-self to blame the 'others' for these behaviors. This is not only not constructive, but is untrue as well.

Since the alters in one's system are not separate people but are aspects of the same person, if arrested for a crime a court of law would not allow one to be released. Rather they would hold the person in total responsible. Therefore, what one does while dissociated is the responsibility of the waking-self, regardless of what those deeds were. This is hard to accept, but a simple truth none-the-less.

If a person wishes to gain complete control of their life, this is one of the most important steps toward achieving that goal, taking total responsibility for one's actions whether dissociated or not.

Author's Personal Perspective:

When I began to work on these issues I felt that I was not responsible for my actions when I was dissociated into someone else. I would tell my therapist that he or she did whatever undesirable deed had been done. This attitude held me prisoner because I needed to understand deep down where it counted that these alternates of mine ARE me. After I accepted this hard truth, I was able to face my alters with more force when it came to holding the reigns on my behavior when I'm dissociated. I have spent much time speaking with those parts of myself involved, explaining the hard truths of the world to them. For instance, some my alters still live in the time in my life when stealing food to survive was necessary. These behaviors are no longer needed, but I have been guilty of stealing food as an adult when dissociated. Once I understood what was happening, I went to them and explained that stealing is not only not needed but it can get us into deep trouble with the law and get us put into prison. I took responsibility for what was taken and admitted my deeds. Luckily, I was not prosecuted.

Taking responsibility for my actions has been a huge leap toward ending the chaos I have lived with all of my life because of the actions of my alters.

Taking Responsibility

Question 1:

Do you believe you are totally responsible for your actions
while dissociated? Why or why not?

Question 2:

Can you name something you have done while dissociated that
you have not taken responsibility for? Something you have
taken responsibility for?

Question 3:

To you, what is the biggest benefit taking responsibility for your
actions, whether dissociated or not, would bring to your life?

Author's Suggestions:

Question 1:

A person's perspective on this subject will change as they go through the recovery process. Eventually, one must maintain responsibility.

Question 2:

- Lies
- Stealing
- Harsh words
- Hitting someone
- Fighting
- Yelling

Question 3:

Gaining control of the chaos that you have lived with all your life.

Integration

The holy grail of recovery for one living with Dissociative Identity Disorder has traditionally been integration. Integration is often understood, by people who don't understand DID thoroughly, as being a pulling together of the alternate personalities into one cohesive personality.

There are two basic problems with this definition.

The first problem is that people who live with this condition have become very accustomed to living with their alters, and often become quite protective of them. In their minds, such a definition sounds like a death sentence to these wonderful creations.

The second problem is that a person living with DID has structural changes in their brains (the amygdalae and hippocampi) caused by the constant secretions of stress hormones that flooded their bodies when they were children and their brains were developing. These structural changes make it impossible for them to become a 'singleton'. (This subject is covered in more depth in the author's book, Becoming: The Wonders of Integration).

Like it is impossible for an adult who is a 'singleton' to become a 'multiple', it is not possible for a person who has matured as a 'multiple' to become a 'singleton'.

Instead, **co-consciousness** and **cooperation/co-consciousness** need to become goals for treatment of this condition. I'm going to spend the next few sections taking about these two important concepts.

Co-consciousness

In the beginning of recovery, one of the most distressing stages is the discovery by alternate personalities to the existence of one another. The waking self may have become aware that they lose time, and understand on some level that it is another personality taking over when they do, but it is important to remember that often the other personalities are not conscious of each other. This allows each personality to have his/her own life and to make decisions on their own that affects the survivor to continue unabated. If these amnesiac walls are allowed to stand between the personalities, the chaos of dissociation will remain.

Breaking down the divisions between personalities is not easy as the person living with DID has spent a lifetime building up and protecting them and will not yield to dropping their defenses easily. It can be clearly seen though, that for the life of the person living with DID to move forward, co-consciousness (aka self-awareness) and sharing of actions between the waking self and the alternates must be established.

One technique to accomplish this goal is to utilize the safe place. The person living with this condition can go to their safe place and initiate conversations, helping the system to understand that taking over the body is not necessary and that doing so causes distress and harm. It takes a great deal of time and effort for the separate parts to accept that their taking over the body is harmful as each one sees it as their right and sometimes they see the waking self as incapable of handling life if they do not. It is up to the waking self to not only stress to the others their desire to be in charge, but also to accept the fact, that they live in the now world and therefore are the most logical personality to be in charge. Once again there can be resistance because the waking self may feel put upon at having to be the personality who must have the final say in all matters, but a great way to keep order in a multiple's system is for the waking self to adopt the motto, "the buck stops here."

Once co-consciousness (awareness) is established life will become more tolerable for the entire system, especially the waking self. Awakening in a strange place, wearing strange clothes, or being accused of saying things not remembered having been said will lessen in frequency. It is then that the person living with DID can start to plan a future, because they are no longer fighting so much against the coping mechanisms of the past.

Author's Personal Perspective

I can remember very well the chaos that existed inside my mind when my alternates and I first discovered one another. I was horrified and I think for the most part so were they. The amnesiac barriers I had erected to protect myself from the horrors of my childhood now stood between me and my ability to have a good life in the now. I couldn't move forward and make a great future for myself because so much of me lived in the past. The chaos of dissociation is hard to understand unless you have lived through it. It is hard to realize that you've lost a day but that the people around you are oblivious to the fact you don't remember what they are speaking of when they bring that day up. I've gotten very good at speaking to people I don't know, but who know me (often by an alternates name) whom I have met during a dissociative episode. They never realize I have just had a very vague conversation with them. It is very hard on a person's sense of stability to have such things happen. Not only this, but one of my personalities has gotten me in trouble with the police. That was very frightening.

I began my journey to co-consciousness on the beach. I would go there and sit with my personalities around a beach fire and talk to them about the importance of them not taking over the body. We talked about triggers, warning signs, and most importantly, my need to be the one who has the final say on all decisions. It has taken a long time and a lot of beach talks, but we have become aware of each other's actions, and we work together for the common good.

Co-Consciousness

Question 1

Name two ways that lack of awareness of each other's actions
in your system has negatively affected your life.

Question 2:

What definition would you give the term co-consciousness?

Question 3:

What resistance have you met, or do you expect to meet, when
you start working on co-consciousness?

Author's Suggestions:

Question 1:

- Visits from the police
- Losing friends
- Losing jobs
- Fear

Question 2:

Awareness between all of the selves of one another.

Question 3:

- Lack of willingness from each personality to break down the amnesiac barriers
- Fear of not being in control by each personality
- Lack of belief that the waking self can handle life situations

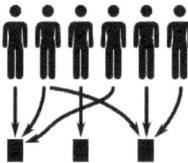

Cooperation and Co-Consciousness

The chaos of living in a mind which is splintered on ideology, with each part wanting to live a separate life, can't be expressed well enough in words to help in the understanding of a person has never experienced it. An analogy that might help is to think of a country where the citizens are very polarized away from one another along lines such as race or religion. One might see how hate and fear can be bred in such a divided country and how, since all parties involved believe they are in the right, wars are begun pitting neighbor against neighbor and brother against brother.

As has been stated, "A house divided against itself cannot stand."

In the system of a multiple there are many facets of the individual who have taken on a life of their own, and each believe they have a right to control their world. They may share important values, but they may have different understandings of how to interact with the outside world.

It is because of this chaos, that cooperation among the different selves should be an important consideration. Again, the safe place is a wonderful place for this cooperation to begin. The opinions of the survivor's alters must be heard, and after careful consideration, needs met.

For instance, a person goes to their safe place to discover why someone in their system has stolen food. In this visit they are told that they stole the item because they were hungry and they didn't trust the waking self to get them some food. Through discussion, the waking self explains the consequences of stealing, and an agreement is reached between them and the alter in question. Then the next time the alter gets anxious because they are hungry, the waking self can get some food as soon as possible, thus allaying this fear. In this way, trust is built between the waking self and the alter. Once trust has been established, through this internal communication, cooperation can begin.

Cooperation among the alters as to how to deal with the outside world and who has the final say in these interactions is a huge step forward for the person living with DID. A leader must emerge from the system, the one for which the buck stops. This is usually the waking self.

Another consequence of cooperation among the alters is what is termed co-consciousness. The best description for co-consciousness is that all the alters are aware of each other's actions, no matter who is in charge. This greatly cuts down on amnesic episodes, and thus the person gains an enormous amount of control over their life. Once this awareness happens, it is much easier to utilize the talents of each personality. In essence, the person goes from a disjointed conglomeration to a unified and cooperative whole.

Author's Personal Perspective:

When I entered therapy, there was no cooperation or good communication within my internal system. As a result, I would lose time and do and say things that I couldn't account for. After I established the beach as my safe place, I began to sit around the beach fire and talk with my alters about what was going on and established a trusting relationship with them. In other words, I established trust with myself. I, as the waking self, became the leader and take full responsibility for all the actions carried out by all of me no matter whether dissociated or not. The greatest gift I received from this new cooperation, was the awareness of what I am doing almost all of the time. We became co-conscious of each other's thoughts, feelings and actions. This has brought me a great deal of peace and healing.

Cooperation and Co-Consciousness

Question 1:

Make a list of the things that are made more difficult because of lack of trust in your system.

Question 2:

In what way can you establish trust and cooperation among your alters?

Question 3:

What do you think would change if you establish co-consciousness within your system?

Author's Suggestions

Question 1:

Just about all things in life are more difficult if you are living in a mind that is divided against itself.

Question 2:

- Talking to them
- Listening to their opinions and fears
- Sitting with them and not saying a word
- Use your imagination

Question 3:

- Peaceful coexistence
- Not losing time
- Not being accused of saying or doing things you don't remember

Moving On

When a person who has lived through severe abuse as a child receives the help they need, there inevitably will come the day when they are ready to move on into the future. This does not mean they forget what happened to them or that they deny their pasts, but rather they make the conscious decision to leave therapy and live as normal lives as they are able, even with the continuing presence of alternate personalities. They have made the important decision to build a future based on who they are rather than on the knowledge of where they come from, an enormous leap of faith forward.

After all the trauma and drama of moving through the process of recovery, leaving therapy and moving on to live life as an ordinary citizen can seem like a wonderful pipe dream. One important thing to keep in mind, therefore, is during the recovery process to be constantly taking stock of what life will be like AFTER the survivor has healed as much as they wish to.

Making a life for oneself with the knowledge of the incurable damages that have been done to one's brain and psyche seems like an impossibility when first entering therapy, but the goal of any good therapist is to make themselves obsolete in the lives of their clients, and persons living with Dissociative Identity Disorder are not the exception to this hope. It is natural for a client with this disorder to form a parental bond with their therapist, but there will come the day when they must fly out of the nest.

Although after therapy survivors can become "just like everyone else" in many ways, they still may find themselves in the position of being more alive and aware then most people around them. They find they enjoy life in a way that most people don't, enjoying the simple things and noticing the beauty around them. They are also often very social conscious, seeing the need all around them and feeling great empathy for the hurting people of their communities and the world.

Author's Perspective:

After twenty-seven arduous years of therapy, I finally found myself ready to move on into life. My therapist had spent many hours preparing me for this step by continually challenging me with the questions, "What will it be like for you to be just an ordinary person?" I knew that I would always be different than others in that I would continue to live with alternate selves, but in the important ways in my interactions with the outside world, I am just like everyone else.

That having been said, I am more alive and alert to things around me than anyone else in my environment. I see the beauty of the stars at night, and feel awe when I look into the eyes of my two-year old nephew. At the same time, I am acutely aware of the social injustices in our society and I try my best to help others by sharing my experiences. These are positive traits I have found in all the multiples I have I contact with on the Internet.

I believe the world needs more multiples because we have so much passion and love to offer.

Moving On

Question 1:

Do you feel you should or can forget your past? Why?

Question 2:

What does being "like everyone else" mean to you?

Question 3:

What things do you notice in your surroundings that are beautiful? That are in need of change?

Author's Suggestions:

Question 1:

Forgetting the past is impossible for anyone to do unless they have a terrible brain injury. One should strive never to forget, but to let it go into the past where it belongs and move on.

Question 2:

This a very personal thing. Your "normal" may not look like mine or anyone else's.

Question 3:

- The stars
- Being alone with a loved one
- The birds singing in the morning
- Hunger
- Want
- Homelessness
- War

Resources for Help

The Ross Institute has two hospitals that treat DID. They are both very good places to go to learn about yourself. I have been in the one in Grand Rapids twice and highly recommend the experience. You can see interviews with Dr. Colin Ross on YouTube. He is the founder and runner of The Colin Ross Institute.

The Ross Institute
1701 Gateway Blvd # 349
Richardson, TX 75080
Phone:(972) 918-9588

University Behavioral Health of Denton
2026 W. University Drive
Denton, Texas 76201
1-940-320-8100
1-888-320-8101

Forest View Hospital
Please call the Forest View Assessment and Referral Center for more information at 1-(800)-949-8439
Del Amo Behavioral Health System
23700 Camino del Sol
Torrance, CA 90505
Phone: (310) 530-1151
Toll Free: (800) 533-5266

There are two online Support Groups that I highly recommend. If you visit tell them Morgan sent you. They'll understand. I received a great deal of love and comfort from the people on these sites.

Ivory Gardens
www.igdid.com
www.igdid.org

Trauma Survivors Support Group
www.ftas.net

Please feel free to check out my blog site:
www.morgan6062.blog

I have written two other books about my experiences living with Dissociative Identity Disorder. Both are available on Amazon in both paperback and Kindle formats.

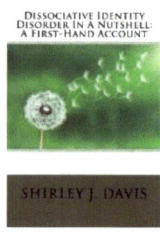

Dissociative Identity Disorder in a Nutshell: A First-Hand Account

Becoming: The Wonders of Integration

www.ingramcontent.com/pod-product-compliance
Lightning Source LLC
Chambersburg PA
CBHW050811290526
45792CB00001B/65